## GRAHAM CRUMB CRUST

1½ c. GRAHAM CRUMBS

⅓ c. SUGAR

⅓ c. MELTED BUTTER

## CHOC

1½ c. CHOC. COOKIES CRUMBS

⅓ c. SUGAR

⅓ c. MELTED BUTTER

## ALMOND CRUMB CRUST

1 c. CHOPPED ALMONDS

¾ c. VANILLA WAFFER CRUMBS

¼ c. SUGAR

¼ c MELTED BUTTER

BAKE 350°F (8-10 MIN.)

# JELL-O®
### BRAND
# CLASSIC RECIPES™

Publications International, Ltd.

Favorite Brand Name Recipes at www.fbnr.com

**Microwave Cooking:** Microwave ovens vary in wattage. Use the cooking times as
guidelines and check for doneness before adding more time.

**Preparation/Cooking Times:** Preparation times are based on the approximate amount
of time required to assemble the recipe before cooking, baking, chilling or serving. These
times include preparation steps such as measuring, chopping and mixing. The fact that
some preparations and cooking can be done simultaneously is taken into account.
Preparation of optional ingredients and serving suggestions is not included.

# Table of Contents

# Memorable Molds

*Nothing looks or tastes quite like a
beautiful gelatin mold! With lively
JELL-O colors and flavors, desserts and
snacks will never be the same.*

# Cranberry Fruit Mold

 2 cups boiling water
 1 package (8-serving size) or 2 packages (4-serving size) JELL-O®
   Brand Cranberry Flavor Gelatin Dessert or JELL-O® Brand
   Cranberry Flavor Sugar Free Low Calorie Gelatin Dessert
 1 1/2 cups cold juice, ginger ale, lemon-lime carbonated beverage,
   seltzer or water
 2 cups halved green and/or red seedless grapes
 1 can (11 ounces) mandarin orange segments, drained

STIR boiling water into gelatin in large bowl at least 2 minutes until completely dissolved. Stir in cold juice. Refrigerate about 1 1/2 hours or until thickened (spoon drawn through leaves definite impression). Stir in fruit. Spoon into 6-cup mold.

REFRIGERATE 4 hours or until firm. Unmold. Garnish as desired.

*Makes 10 servings*

**Preparation Time:** 15 minutes
**Refrigerating Time:** 5 1/2 hours

# Apple Blossom Mold

1 $\frac{1}{2}$ cups boiling water

1 package (8-serving size) or 2 packages (4-serving size each)
JELL-O® Brand Lemon Flavor Gelatin

2 cups cold apple juice

1 cup diced red and green apples

STIR boiling water into gelatin in large bowl at least 2 minutes until completely dissolved. Stir in cold juice. Refrigerate about 1 $\frac{1}{2}$ hours or until thickened (spoon drawn through leaves definite impression). Stir in apples. Pour into 6-cup mold which has been sprayed with no stick cooking spray.

REFRIGERATE 4 hours or until firm. Unmold. Garnish as desired.

*Makes 10 servings*

**Variation:** Sugar Free Low Calorie Gelatin may be substituted.

**Preparation Time:** 15 minutes
**Refrigerating Time:** 5 $\frac{1}{2}$ hours

*Apple Blossom Mold*

# Ambrosia Mold

1 can (8 ounces) crushed pineapple in juice, undrained
2 cups boiling water
1 package (8-serving size) or 2 packages (4-serving size) JELL-O®
   Brand Orange Flavor Gelatin Dessert
1 3/4 cups thawed COOL WHIP® Whipped Topping
1 can (11 ounces) mandarin orange segments, drained
1 1/2 cups miniature marshmallows
1/2 cup BAKER'S ANGEL FLAKE® Coconut (optional)

DRAIN pineapple, reserving juice. Add cold water to juice to make 1 cup.

STIR boiling water into gelatin in large bowl at least 2 minutes until completely dissolved. Stir in measured pineapple juice and water. Refrigerate about 1 1/4 hours or until slightly thickened (consistency of unbeaten egg whites).

STIR in whipped topping with wire whisk until smooth. Refrigerate 10 minutes or until mixture will mound. Stir in pineapple, oranges, marshmallows and coconut. Spoon into 6-cup mold.

REFRIGERATE 3 hours or until firm. Unmold.     *Makes 10 servings*

**Preparation Time:** 15 minutes
**Refrigerating Time:** 4 1/2 hours

# Cranberry Cream Cheese Mold

1 1/2 cups boiling water

1 package (8-serving size) or 2 packages (4-serving size) JELL-O®
   Brand Cranberry Flavor Gelatin Dessert, or any red flavor

1 1/2 cups cold water

1/2 teaspoon ground cinnamon

1 medium apple, chopped

1 cup whole berry cranberry sauce

1 package (8 ounces) PHILADELPHIA® Cream Cheese, softened

STIR boiling water into gelatin in large bowl at least 2 minutes until completely dissolved. Stir in cold water and cinnamon. Reserve 1 cup gelatin at room temperature. Refrigerate remaining gelatin about 1 1/2 hours or until thickened (spoon drawn through leaves definite impression).

STIR apple and cranberry sauce into thickened gelatin. Spoon into 6-cup mold. Refrigerate about 30 minutes or until set but not firm (gelatin should stick to finger when touched and should mound).

STIR reserved 1 cup gelatin gradually into cream cheese in medium bowl with wire whisk until smooth. Pour over gelatin layer in mold.

REFRIGERATE 4 hours or until firm. Unmold. Garnish as desired.

*Makes 12 servings*

**Note:** To prepare without cream cheese layer, omit cream cheese. Refrigerate all of the gelatin about 1 1/2 hours or until thickened. Stir in apple and cranberry sauce. Pour into mold. Refrigerate.

**Preparation Time:** 20 minutes
**Refrigerating Time:** 6 hours

# Gazpacho Salad

1 cup diced tomato

¹/₂ cup diced peeled cucumber

¹/₄ cup diced green pepper

2 tablespoons diced red pepper

2 tablespoons thinly sliced green onion

2 tablespoons vinegar

¹/₄ teaspoon pepper

¹/₈ teaspoon garlic powder (optional)

1¹/₂ cups tomato juice

1 package (4-serving size) JELL-O® Brand Lemon Flavor Sugar
Free Low Calorie Gelatin Dessert or JELL-O® Brand Lemon
Flavor Gelatin Dessert

Crackers (optional)

MIX vegetables, vinegar, pepper and garlic powder, if desired, in medium bowl; set aside. Bring tomato juice to boil in small saucepan. Stir into gelatin in large bowl at least 2 minutes until completely dissolved. Refrigerate about 1¹/₄ hours or until slightly thickened (consistency of unbeaten egg whites).

STIR in vegetable mixture. Pour into 4-cup mold.

REFRIGERATE 3 hours or until firm. Unmold. Serve with crackers, if desired. Garnish as desired. *Makes 6 servings*

**Preparation Time:** 20 minutes
**Refrigerating Time:** 4¹/₄ hours

*Gazpacho Salad*

# Juicy Layered Orange Pineapple Mold

1 can (20 ounces) crushed pineapple in juice, undrained
Cold orange juice
1 1/2 cups boiling water
1 package (8-serving size) or 2 packages (4-serving size each)
JELL-O® Brand Orange Flavor Gelatin
1 package (8 ounces) PHILADELPHIA® Cream Cheese, softened

DRAIN pineapple, reserving juice. Add cold orange juice to pineapple juice to make 1 1/2 cups. Stir boiling water into gelatin in large bowl at least 2 minutes until completely dissolved. Stir in measured juice. Reserve 1 cup gelatin at room temperature.

STIR 1/2 of the crushed pineapple into remaining gelatin. Pour into 6-cup mold which has been sprayed with no stick cooking spray. Refrigerate about 2 hours or until set but not firm (should stick to finger when touched and should mound).

STIR reserved gelatin gradually into cream cheese in medium bowl with wire whisk until smooth. Stir in remaining crushed pineapple. Spoon over gelatin layer in mold.

REFRIGERATE 4 hours or until firm. Unmold. Garnish as desired.

*Makes 10 servings*

**Take a Shortcut:** Soften cream cheese in microwave on HIGH 15 to 20 seconds.

**Preparation Time:** 20 minutes
**Refrigerating Time:** 6 hours

*Juicy Layered Orange Pineapple Mold*

# "Red, White and Blue" Mold

2³/₄ cups boiling water

1 package (4-serving size) JELL-O® Brand Strawberry Flavor
   Gelatin Dessert, or any red flavor

1 package (4-serving size) JELL-O® Brand Berry Blue Flavor
   Gelatin Dessert

1 cup cold water

1¹/₂ cups sliced strawberries

1 package (4-serving size) JELL-O® Brand Lemon Flavor Gelatin
   Dessert

1 pint (2 cups) vanilla ice cream, softened

1¹/₂ cups blueberries

STIR 1 cup of the boiling water into each of the red and blue gelatins in separate medium bowls at least 2 minutes until completely dissolved. Stir ¹/₂ cup of the cold water into each bowl.

PLACE bowl of red gelatin in larger bowl of ice and water. Stir until thickened, about 8 minutes. Stir in strawberries. Pour into 9×5-inch loaf pan. Refrigerate 7 minutes.

MEANWHILE, stir remaining ³/₄ cup boiling water into lemon gelatin in medium bowl at least 2 minutes until completely dissolved. Spoon in ice cream until melted and smooth. Spoon over red gelatin in pan. Refrigerate 7 minutes.

MEANWHILE, place bowl of blue gelatin in larger bowl of ice and water. Stir until thickened, about 7 minutes. Stir in blueberries. Spoon over lemon gelatin in pan. Refrigerate 4 hours or until firm. Unmold. Garnish as desired.                                    *Makes 12 servings*

**Preparation Time:** 45 minutes
**Refrigerating Time:** 4¹/₂ hours

*"Red, White and Blue" Mold*

# Creamy Cantaloupe

1 medium cantaloupe (about 3$^1$/$_2$ pounds)
$^3$/$_4$ cup boiling water
1 package (4-serving size) JELL-O® Brand Gelatin, any flavor
$^1$/$_2$ cup cold orange juice
$^1$/$_2$ cup thawed COOL WHIP® Whipped Topping

CUT melon in half lengthwise; remove seeds. Scoop out melon, leaving about 1-inch-thick border of melon. Dice scooped out melon. Drain well. Cut thin slice from bottom of each melon shell to allow shells to stand upright, or place in small bowls.

STIR boiling water into gelatin in large bowl at least 2 minutes until completely dissolved. Stir in cold juice. Refrigerate 15 minutes or until slightly thickened (consistency of unbeaten egg whites). Gently stir in whipped topping. Stir in reserved diced melon. Pour into melon shells.

REFRIGERATE 3 hours or until firm. Cut into wedges.

*Makes 8 servings*

**Preparation Time:** 15 minutes
**Refrigerating Time:** 3 hours

*Creamy Cantaloupe*

# Crown Jewel Dessert

> 1 package (4-serving size) JELL-O® Brand Lime Flavor Gelatin Dessert*
>
> 1 package (4-serving size) JELL-O® Brand Orange Flavor Gelatin Dessert*
>
> 1 package (4-serving size) JELL-O® Brand Strawberry Flavor Gelatin Dessert*
>
> 3 cups boiling water
>
> 1 1/2 cups cold water
>
> 1 cup boiling water
>
> 1 package (4-serving size) JELL-O® Brand Strawberry Flavor Gelatin Dessert
>
> 1/2 cup cold water
>
> 1 tub (8 ounces) COOL WHIP® Whipped Topping, thawed

*Or use any 3 different flavors of JELL-O Brand Gelatin Dessert.*

PREPARE lime, orange and 1 package strawberry gelatin separately as directed on packages, using 1 cup boiling water and 1/2 cup cold water for each. Pour each flavor into separate 8-inch square pans. Refrigerate 4 hours or until firm. Cut into 1/2-inch cubes; measure 1 1/2 cups of each flavor. (Use the remaining gelatin cubes for garnish, if desired, or for snacking.)

STIR 1 cup boiling water into remaining package of strawberry gelatin in medium bowl at least 2 minutes until completely dissolved. Stir in 1/2 cup cold water. Refrigerate 45 minutes or until slightly thickened (consistency of unbeaten egg whites).

STIR in ½ of the whipped topping. Gently stir in measured gelatin cubes. Pour into 9×5-inch loaf pan.

REFRIGERATE 4 hours or until firm. Unmold. Garnish with remaining whipped topping and gelatin cubes, if desired.

*Makes 16 servings*

**Preparation Time:** 45 minutes
**Refrigerating Time:** 8¾ hours

*Crown Jewel Dessert*

# Rainbow Ribbon Mold

6¼ cups boiling water

    5 packages (4-serving size) JELL-O® Brand Gelatin Dessert, any
        5 different flavors

    1 cup (½ pint) BREAKSTONE'S® Sour Cream or BREYERS®
        Vanilla Lowfat Yogurt

STIR 1¼ cups boiling water into 1 flavor of gelatin in small bowl at least 2 minutes until completely dissolved. Pour ¾ cup of the dissolved gelatin into 6-cup ring mold. Refrigerate about 15 minutes until set but not firm (gelatin should stick to finger when touched and should mound). Refrigerate remaining gelatin in bowl about 5 minutes until slightly thickened (consistency of unbeaten egg whites). Gradually stir in 3 tablespoons of the sour cream. Spoon over gelatin in pan. Refrigerate about 15 minutes or until set but not firm (gelatin should stick to finger when touched and should mound).

MEANWHILE, repeat process with each remaining gelatin flavor. (Be sure to cool dissolved gelatin to room temperature before pouring into mold.) Refrigerate gelatin as directed to create a total of 10 alternating clear and creamy gelatin layers.

REFRIGERATE 2 hours or until firm. Unmold. Garnish as desired.

*Makes 12 servings*

**Preparation Time:** 1 hour
**Refrigerating Time:** 4½ hours

*Rainbow Ribbon Mold*

# Creamy Fruited Mold

1 cup boiling water
1 package (4-serving size) JELL-O® Brand Gelatin Dessert, any
    flavor
1 cup cold water or apple juice
1½ cups thawed COOL WHIP® Whipped Topping
1 cup diced fruit

STIR boiling water into gelatin in medium bowl at least 2 minutes until completely dissolved. Stir in cold water. Refrigerate about 1¼ hours or until slightly thickened (consistency of unbeaten egg whites). Gently stir in whipped topping. Refrigerate about 15 minutes or until thickened (spoon drawn through leaves definite impression). Stir in fruit. Pour into 5-cup mold.

REFRIGERATE 4 hours or until firm. Unmold. Garnish as desired.

*Makes 8 servings*

**Preparation Time:** 15 minutes
**Refrigerating Time:** 5½ hours

*Creamy Fruited Mold*

# Creamy Fruited Lime Salad

1 1/2 cups boiling water

1 package (8-serving size) or 2 packages (4-serving size) JELL-O®
Brand Lime Flavor Gelatin Dessert

1 can (8 ounces) crushed pineapple in juice, undrained

1 cup LIGHT N' LIVELY® 1% Lowfat Cottage Cheese with
Calcium

1 package (8 ounces) PHILADELPHIA® Cream Cheese, softened

1 cup thawed COOL WHIP® Whipped Topping

1/2 cup chopped walnuts

1/4 cup chopped maraschino cherries

Salad greens (optional)

STIR boiling water into gelatin in large bowl at least 2 minutes until
completely dissolved. Stir in pineapple with juice. Refrigerate about
1 1/4 hours or until slightly thickened (consistency of unbeaten egg whites).

STIR cottage cheese into cream cheese in separate bowl until well
blended. Gently stir in whipped topping until smooth. Beat into slightly
thickened gelatin with wire whisk until well blended. Stir in walnuts and
cherries. Pour into 6-cup mold.

REFRIGERATE 4 hours or until firm. Unmold. Serve on salad greens,
if desired.                                              *Makes 12 servings*

**Preparation Time:** 15 minutes
**Refrigerating Time:** 5 1/4 hours

# Cucumber Sour Cream Mold

1 ½ cups boiling water

  1 package (8-serving size) *or* 2 packages (4-serving size) JELL-O®
     Brand Lime Flavor Gelatin Dessert

 ¼ teaspoon salt

1 ½ cups cold water

  1 tablespoon lemon juice

 ½ cup MIRACLE WHIP® Salad Dressing

 ½ cup BREAKSTONE'S® Sour Cream

1 ½ cups chopped seeded peeled cucumber

  2 tablespoons minced onion

  1 teaspoon dill weed

STIR boiling water into gelatin and salt in large bowl at least 2 minutes until completely dissolved. Stir in cold water and lemon juice. Refrigerate about 1 ¼ hours or until slightly thickened (consistency of unbeaten egg whites).

MIX salad dressing and sour cream in small bowl until well blended. Stir into thickened gelatin. Refrigerate about 15 minutes or until thickened (spoon drawn through leaves definite impression). Stir in cucumber, onion and dill weed. Pour into 5-cup mold.

REFRIGERATE 4 hours or until firm. Unmold. Garnish as desired.

*Makes 10 servings*

**Preparation Time:** 15 minutes
**Refrigerating Time:** 5 ½ hours

# Perfect Pies and Cakes

*Add the ideal finish to a meal with a spectacular pie or cake creation. These favorites are sure to please, and they'll be long-remembered.*

# Cool 'n' Easy® Pie

    ²/₃ cup boiling water
    1 package (4-serving size) JELL-O® Brand Gelatin, any flavor
    ¹/₂ cup cold juice, any flavor
       Ice cubes
    1 tub (8 ounces) COOL WHIP® Whipped Topping, thawed
    1 prepared graham cracker crumb crust (6 ounces)
       Assorted fruit (optional)

STIR boiling water into gelatin in large bowl 2 minutes or until
completely dissolved. Mix cold juice and ice to make 1 cup. Add to
gelatin, stirring until slightly thickened. Remove any remaining ice.

STIR in whipped topping with wire whisk until smooth. Refrigerate
10 to 15 minutes or until mixture is very thick and will mound. Spoon
into crust.

REFRIGERATE 4 hours or until firm. Just before serving, garnish with
fruit, if desired. Store leftover pie in refrigerator.          *Makes 8 servings*

# Double Layer Chocolate Pie

$^1/_2$ **package (4 ounces) PHILADELPHIA® Cream Cheese, softened**

1 **tablespoon milk or half-and-half**

1 **tablespoon sugar**

1 **tub (8 ounces) COOL WHIP® Whipped Topping, thawed**

1 **prepared chocolate flavor crumb crust (6 ounces)**

2 **cups cold milk or half-and-half**

2 **packages (4-serving size) JELL-O® Chocolate Flavor Instant Pudding & Pie Filling**

MIX cream cheese, 1 tablespoon milk and sugar in large bowl with wire whisk until smooth. Gently stir in $1^1/_2$ cups of the whipped topping. Spread onto bottom of crust.

POUR 2 cups milk into bowl. Add pudding mixes. Beat with wire whisk until well mixed. (Mixture will be thick.) Immediately stir in remaining whipped topping. Spread over cream cheese layer.

REFRIGERATE 4 hours or until set. Garnish as desired.

*Makes 8 servings*

**Tip:** To quickly soften cream cheese, microwave on HIGH for 15 to 20 seconds.

**Preparation Time:** 15 minutes
**Refrigerating Time:** 4 hours

*Double Layer Chocolate Pie*

# Pudding Poke Cake

1 package (2-layer size) chocolate cake mix or cake mix with
   pudding in the mix
4 cups cold milk
2 packages (4-serving size) JELL-O® Vanilla Flavor Instant
   Pudding & Pie Filling

PREPARE and bake cake mix as directed on package for 13×9-inch baking pan. Remove from oven. Immediately poke holes down through cake to pan at 1-inch intervals with round handle of a wooden spoon. (Or, poke holes with a plastic drinking straw, using turning motion to make large holes.)

POUR milk into large bowl. Add pudding mixes. Beat with wire whisk 2 minutes. Quickly pour about ½ of the thin pudding mixture evenly over warm cake and into holes. Let remaining pudding mixture stand to thicken slightly. Spoon over top of cake, swirling to frost cake.

REFRIGERATE at least 1 hour or until ready to serve.

*Makes 15 servings*

**Preparation Time:** 30 minutes
**Baking Time:** 40 minutes
**Refrigerating Time:** 1 hour

# Frozen Coffee Pie

$^1/_2$ cup hot fudge sauce

1 prepared chocolate flavor crumb crust (6 ounces or 9 inches)

$1^3/_4$ cups cold milk

2 packages (4-serving size each) JELL-O® Vanilla Flavor Instant Pudding & Pie Filling

2 tablespoons MAXWELL HOUSE® Instant Coffee, any variety

1 tub (8 ounces) COOL WHIP® Whipped Topping, thawed

HEAT hot fudge sauce as directed on jar. Pour into crust, tilting to cover bottom. Freeze 5 minutes.

POUR milk into large bowl. Add pudding mixes and instant coffee.

BEAT with wire whisk 1 minute or until well blended. Gently stir in whipped topping. Spoon into crust.

FREEZE 4 hours or until firm. Remove from freezer. Let stand 10 minutes before serving. Garnish with additional whipped topping, if desired.                     *Makes 8 servings*

**Great Substitute:** For a delicious Frozen Mocha Mud Pie variation, substitute JELL-O Chocolate Flavor Instant Pudding & Pie Filling for the Vanilla Flavor.

**Preparation Time:** 15 minutes
**Freezing Time:** 4 hours

# No Bake Pineapple-Ginger Cheesecake Squares

1 package (11.1 ounces) JELL-O® No Bake Real Cheesecake
2 tablespoons sugar
1 tablespoon water
6 tablespoons butter or margarine, melted
1 1/2 teaspoons ground ginger
1 can (20 ounces) crushed pineapple in juice, well drained, divided
1 1/2 cups cold milk
1 teaspoon grated lemon peel

MIX Crust Mix, sugar, water, butter and ginger thoroughly with fork in 9×9-inch pan until crumbs are well moistened. Reserve 2 tablespoons. Press firmly onto bottom of pan using dry measuring cup. Spread 1/2 of the pineapple on the crust.

BEAT milk, Filling Mix and lemon peel with electric mixer on low speed until blended. Beat on medium speed 3 minutes. (Filling will be thick.) Spoon over pineapple in crust.

REFRIGERATE at least 1 hour. Top with remaining pineapple and reserved crumbs. Store leftover cheesecake, covered, in refrigerator.

*Makes 8 servings*

**Great Substitute:** Orange peel can be substituted for lemon peel.

**Preparation Time:** 10 minutes
**Refrigerating Time:** 1 hour

*No Bake Pineapple-Ginger Cheesecake Square*

# White Chocolate-Hazelnut Pie

2 cups cold milk

2 packages (4-serving size each) JELL-O® White Chocolate Flavor or other Chocolate Flavor Instant Pudding & Pie Filling

1 envelope (.64 ounces) GENERAL FOODS INTERNATIONAL COFFEES® Hazelnut Flavor (about 2 tablespoons)

1 tub (8 ounces) COOL WHIP® Whipped Topping, thawed, divided

1 prepared chocolate flavor or graham cracker crumb crust (6 ounces or 9 inches)

POUR milk into medium bowl. Add pudding mixes and flavored instant coffee. Beat with wire whisk 1 minute or until well blended. (Mixture will be thick.) Gently stir in ¹/₂ of the whipped topping. Spoon evenly into crust. Spread remaining whipped topping over pudding in crust.

REFRIGERATE 3 hours or until set. Garnish as desired.

*Makes 8 servings*

**Preparation Time:** 15 minutes
**Refrigerating Time:** 3 hours

*White Chocolate-Hazelnut Pie*

# Pinwheel Cake and Cream

2 cups cold milk

1 package (4-serving size) JELL-O® Vanilla or French Vanilla
   Flavor Instant Pudding & Pie Filling

1 cup thawed COOL WHIP® Whipped Topping

1 small peach or nectarine, chopped

1 teaspoon grated orange peel

1 package (12 ounces) pound cake, cut into slices

2 cups summer fruits, such as sliced peaches, nectarines or plums;
   seedless grapes; strawberries, raspberries, or blueberries

POUR milk into large bowl. Add pudding mix. Beat with wire whisk
1 minute. Gently stir in whipped topping, chopped peach and grated peel.

ARRANGE pound cake slices on serving plate. Spoon pudding mixture
evenly over cake. Top with fruits. Serve immediately or cover and refrigerate
until ready to serve.                              *Makes 10 servings*

**Preparation Time:** 15 minutes

*Pinwheel Cake and Cream*

# Chocolate Swirl Cheesecake

1 package (11.1 ounces) JELL-O® No Bake Real Cheesecake

2 tablespoons sugar

1/3 cup butter *or* margarine, melted

2 squares BAKER'S® Semi-Sweet Baking Chocolate

1 1/2 cups cold milk, divided

STIR Crust Mix, sugar, melted butter and water thoroughly with fork in 8- or 9-inch pie plate until crumbs are well moistened. First, press mixture firmly against side of pie plate, using finger or large spoon to shape edge. Press remaining crumbs firmly onto bottom of pie plate using measuring cup.

MICROWAVE chocolate and 2 tablespoons of the milk in microwavable bowl on HIGH 1 1/2 minutes or until chocolate is almost melted. Stir until chocolate is completely melted.

POUR cold milk into medium bowl. Add Filling Mix. Beat with electric mixer on lowest speed until blended. Beat on medium speed 3 minutes. (Filling will be thick.) Stir 1/4 cup of the filling into melted chocolate until well blended. Spoon remaining filling into crust. Place spoonfuls of chocolate mixture over filling in crust. Cut through cheesecake filling with knife several times to marbleize.

REFRIGERATE at least 1 hour. Garnish as desired. Store leftover cheesecake in refrigerator. *Makes 8 servings*

**How To Serve:** For ease in serving, dip bottom of pie plate in hot water for 10 to 15 seconds prior to slicing.

**Special Extras:** Garnish cheesecake with additional melted BAKER'S® Semi-Sweet Baking Chocolate drizzle on top. To melt chocolate, place 1 square chocolate in heavy-duty zipper-style plastic sandwich bag. Seal bag tightly. Microwave on HIGH about 1 minute or until chocolate is melted. Fold down top of bag and snip a tiny (about 1/8-inch) piece off 1 corner. Holding top of bag firmly, drizzle chocolate over cheesecake.

**Preparation Time:** 15 minutes
**Refrigerating Time:** 1 hour

# Lemon-Blueberry Pie Cups

6 vanilla wafer cookies

$^3/_4$ cup canned blueberry pie filling

1 cup boiling water

1 package (4-serving size) JELL-O® Brand Lemon Flavor Gelatin

$^3/_4$ cup cold water

$^1/_2$ tub (8 ounces) COOL WHIP® Whipped Topping, thawed

PLACE one vanilla wafer on bottom of each of 6 dessert cups. Top each wafer with 2 tablespoons pie filling. Set aside.

STIR boiling water into gelatin in large bowl at least 2 minutes until completely dissolved.

STIR in cold water. Refrigerate 10 to 15 minutes or until mixture is slightly thickened (consistency of unbeaten egg whites). Stir in $^1/_2$ of the whipped topping until well blended. Spoon over pie filling in cups.

REFRIGERATE 2 hours or until firm. Garnish with remaining whipped topping, if desired. *Makes 6 servings*

**Great Substitutes:** Try using cherry or pineapple pie filling instead of the blueberry pie filling.

**Best of the Season:** Garnish each serving with fresh berries, if desired.

**Preparation Time:** 15 minutes
**Refrigerating Time:** $2^1/_4$ hours

*Lemon-Blueberry Pie Cups*

# Summer Berry Pie

$^3/_4$ cup sugar

3 tablespoons cornstarch

1 $^1/_2$ cups water

1 package (4-serving size) JELL-O® Brand Gelatin Dessert, any
red flavor

1 cup blueberries

1 cup raspberries

1 cup sliced strawberries

1 prepared graham cracker crumb crust (6 ounces)

2 cups thawed COOL WHIP® Whipped Topping

MIX sugar and cornstarch in medium saucepan. Gradually stir in water until smooth. Stirring constantly, cook on medium heat until mixture comes to boil; boil 1 minute. Remove from heat. Stir in gelatin until completely dissolved. Cool to room temperature. Stir in berries. Pour into crust.

REFRIGERATE 3 hours or until firm. Top with whipped topping.

*Makes 8 servings*

**Preparation Time:** 20 minutes

**Refrigerating Time:** 3 hours

*Summer Berry Pie*

# Triple Layer Butterscotch Pie

2 squares BAKER'S® Semi-Sweet Baking Chocolate, melted

1/4 cup sweetened condensed milk

1 prepared chocolate flavor crumb crust (6 ounces or 9 inches)

3/4 cup chopped pecans, toasted

1 3/4 cups cold milk

2 packages (4-serving size each) JELL-O® Butterscotch Flavor
Instant Pudding & Pie Filling

1 tub (8 ounces) COOL WHIP® Whipped Topping, thawed,
divided

POUR chocolate and sweetened condensed milk into bowl; stir until smooth. Pour into crust. Press nuts evenly onto chocolate in crust. Refrigerate 10 minutes.

POUR milk into large bowl. Add pudding mixes. Beat with wire whisk 1 minute or until well blended. (Mixture will be thick.) Spread 1 1/2 cups of the pudding over chocolate in crust. Immediately stir 1/2 of the whipped topping into remaining pudding. Spread over pudding in crust. Top with remaining whipped topping.

REFRIGERATE 3 hours or until set. Garnish as desired.

*Makes 8 servings*

**Great Substitue:** If you are a chocolate lover, simply substitute Chocolate Flavor Pudding for the Butterscotch Flavor.

**Refrigerating Time:** 3 hours

*Triple Layer Butterscotch Pie*

# Lemon Soufflé Cheesecake

1 graham cracker, crushed, or 2 tablespoons graham cracker
   crumbs, divided

²/₃ cup boiling water

1 package (4-serving size) JELL-O® Brand Lemon Flavor Sugar
   Free Low Calorie Gelatin Dessert or JELL-O® Brand Lemon
   Flavor Gelatin Dessert

1 cup LIGHT N' LIVELY® 1% Lowfat Cottage Cheese with
   Calcium

1 tub (8 ounces) PHILADELPHIA® LIGHT® Light Cream
   Cheese

2 cups thawed COOL WHIP FREE® or COOL WHIP LITE®
   Whipped Topping

SPRINKLE ¹/₂ of the crumbs onto side of 8- or 9-inch springform pan
or 9-inch pie plate that has been sprayed with no stick cooking spray.

STIR boiling water into gelatin in large bowl at least 2 minutes until
completely dissolved. Pour into blender container. Add cheeses; cover.
Blend on medium speed until smooth, scraping down sides occasionally.

POUR into large bowl. Gently stir in whipped topping. Pour into
prepared pan; smooth top. Sprinkle remaining crumbs around outside
edge. Refrigerate 4 hours or until set.

REMOVE side of pan just before serving. Garnish as desired.

*Makes 8 servings*

**Preparation Time:** 20 minutes
**Refrigerating Time:** 4 hours

*Lemon Soufflé Cheesecake*

# Ice Cream Shop Pie

1 1/2 cups cold milk, half-and-half or light cream
1 package (4-serving size) JELL-O® Instant Pudding & Pie Filling
1 tub (8 ounces) COOL WHIP® Whipped Topping, thawed
1 prepared crumb crust (6 ounces)

POUR milk into large bowl. Add pudding mix. Beat with wire whisk
2 minutes. Gently stir in whipped topping. Spoon into crust.

FREEZE 6 hours or overnight until firm. Let stand at room temperature
or in refrigerator 15 minutes or until pie can be cut easily.

GARNISH as desired.                                    *Makes 8 servings*

**Cookies-and-Cream Pie:** Use JELL-O® Vanilla Flavor Instant Pudding
& Pie Filling and chocolate crumb crust. Stir in 1 cup chopped chocolate
sandwich cookies with whipped topping.

**Rocky Road Pie:** Use JELL-O® Chocolate Flavor Instant Pudding & Pie
Filling and chocolate crumb crust. Stir in 1/3 cup each BAKER'S® Semi-
Sweet Real Chocolate Chips, miniature marshmallows and chopped nuts
with whipped topping. Serve with chocolate sauce, if desired.

**Peanut Butter Pie:** Use JELL-O® Vanilla Flavor Instant Pudding & Pie
Filling and graham cracker crumb crust. Reduce milk to 1 cup and add
1/2 cup peanut butter with pudding mix. Serve with chocolate sauce and
chopped peanuts, if desired.

**Preparation Time:** 15 minutes
**Freezing Time:** 6 hours

# Gelatin Poke Cake

1 package (2-layer size) white cake mix or cake mix with pudding
    in the mix
1 cup boiling water
1 package (4-serving size) JELL-O® Brand Gelatin Dessert, any
    flavor
1/2 cup cold water
1 tub (8 ounces) COOL WHIP® Whipped Topping, thawed

HEAT oven to 350°F.

PREPARE and bake cake mix as directed on package for 13×9-inch baking pan. Remove from oven. Cool cake in pan 15 minutes. Pierce cake with large fork at 1/2-inch intervals.

MEANWHILE, stir boiling water into gelatin in medium bowl at least 2 minutes until completely dissolved. Stir in cold water; carefully pour over cake. Refrigerate 3 hours.

FROST with whipped topping. Refrigerate at least 1 hour or until ready to serve. Decorate as desired. *Makes 15 servings*

**Preparation Time:** 15 minutes
**Baking Time:** 35 minutes
**Refrigerating Time:** 4 hours

# Fruity Pound Cake

1 package (4-serving size) JELL-O® Brand Lemon Flavor Gelatin
    Dessert

1 teaspoon grated lemon or orange peel

1 package (2-layer size) white cake mix or cake mix with pudding
    in the mix

³/₄ cup water

¹/₄ cup oil

4 eggs

    Fluffy Pudding Frosting (recipe follows)

MIX gelatin, grated peel and cake mix in large bowl.

PREPARE and bake cake mix as directed on package in two 8- or 9-inch
round cake pans. Cool 15 minutes; remove from pans. Cool completely
on wire racks. Fill and frost with Fluffy Pudding Frosting. Decorate as
desired. *Makes 12 servings*

**Fluffy Pudding Frosting:** Pour 1 cup cold milk into medium bowl. Add
1 package (4-serving size) JELL-O® Instant Pudding & Pie Filling, any
flavor, and ¹/₄ cup powdered sugar. Beat with wire whisk 2 minutes. Gently
stir in 1 tub (8 ounces) COOL WHIP® Whipped Topping, thawed. Spread
onto cake at once. Makes about 4 cups or enough for two 8- or 9-inch
layers.

**Preparation Time:** 30 minutes
**Baking Time:** 40 minutes

*Fruity Pound Cake*

# Traditional Kid Treats

*Delight kids of all ages with these fun JELL-O goodies. Make plenty and serve them as snacks. Your kids will keep coming back for more!*

# Cool Sandwich Snacks

10 whole graham crackers or chocolate-flavor graham crackers
$^1\!/_2$ cup chocolate fudge sauce
1 tub (8 ounces) COOL WHIP® Whipped Topping, thawed
   Suggested Garnishes: Multi-colored sprinkles, assorted candies,
   finely crushed cookies, chocolate chunks, chopped nuts or
   toasted BAKER'S ANGEL FLAKE® Coconut

SPREAD $^1\!/_2$ of the graham crackers lightly with chocolate sauce. Spread whipped topping about $^3\!/_4$ inch thick on remaining $^1\!/_2$ of the graham crackers. Press crackers together lightly, making sandwiches. Roll or lightly press edges in suggested garnish.

FREEZE 4 hours or overnight. *Makes 10 sandwiches*

**Make Ahead:** This recipe can be made up to 2 weeks ahead. Wrap well with plastic wrap and freeze.

**Preparation Time:** 15 minutes
**Freezing Time:** 4 hours

# Cool Yogurt Smoothie

1 container (8 ounces) BREYERS® Strawberry Lowfat Yogurt, any variety

$^1/_2$ tub (8 ounces) COOL WHIP® Whipped Topping, thawed or frozen

1 cup fresh or frozen strawberries or any other seasonal fruit, chopped (optional)

PLACE yogurt, whipped topping and fruit in blender container; cover. Blend until smooth. (For thinner consistency, add ice cubes.) Serve immediately. *Makes 2 servings*

**Storage Know-How:** Smoothie can be covered and stored in the refrigerator up to 24 hours, or frozen up to 1 week. Reblend before serving. (Thaw frozen smoothie 20 minutes before blending.)

**Preparation Time:** 1 minute

# Creamy Orange Shake

1 cup cold milk

1 cup orange juice

1 package (4-serving size) JELL-O® Brand Orange Flavor Gelatin Dessert

1 cup vanilla ice cream

POUR milk and juice into blender container. Add gelatin and ice cream; cover. Blend on high speed 30 seconds or until smooth. Serve immediately. *Makes 4 servings*

**Preparation Time:** 5 minutes

*Cool Yogurt Smoothies*

# Dirt Cups

1 package (16 ounces) chocolate sandwich cookies

2 cups cold milk

1 package (4-serving size) JELL-O® Chocolate Flavor Instant
Pudding & Pie Filling

1 tub (8 ounces) COOL WHIP® Whipped Topping, thawed

8 to 10 (7-ounce) paper or plastic cups

Suggested garnishes: gummy worms or other gummy candies,
candy flowers, chopped peanuts, granola

CRUSH cookies in zipper-style plastic bag with rolling pin or in food
processor.

POUR milk into large bowl. Add pudding mix. Beat with wire whisk
2 minutes. Stir in whipped topping and $1/2$ of the crushed cookies.

PLACE about 1 tablespoon of the crushed cookies in each cup. Fill cups
about $3/4$ full with pudding mixture. Top with remaining crushed cookies.

REFRIGERATE until ready to serve. Garnish as desired.

*Makes 8 to 10 servings*

**Sand Cups:** Use 1 package (12 ounces) vanilla wafer cookies and JELL-O®
Vanilla Flavor Instant Pudding & Pie Filling.

**Preparation Time:** 15 minutes

**Refrigerating Time:** 2 hours

*Left to Right: Sand Cups and Dirt Cups*

# Cherry Cola Parfaits

2$\frac{1}{2}$ cups boiling carbonated cola beverage

2 packages (8-serving size each) or 4 packages (4-serving size each)
JELL-O® Brand Cherry Flavor Gelatin

1 tub (8 ounces) COOL WHIP® Whipped Topping, thawed

STIR boiling beverage into gelatin in large bowl at least 2 minutes until completely dissolved. Pour into 13×9-inch pan. Refrigerate at least 3 hours or until firm. Dip bottom of pan in warm water about 15 seconds. Cut into $\frac{1}{2}$-inch cubes.

LAYER gelatin cubes and whipped topping, in alternating layers, into 6 dessert glasses. Garnish with additional whipped topping, if desired.

*Makes 6 servings*

**Take a Shortcut:** For an even quicker version, pour gelatin directly into 6 dessert glasses; refrigerate 3 hours or until set. Top with whipped topping.

**Preparation Time:** 10 minutes
**Refrigerating Time:** 3 hours

# Cosmic Clouds

1 tub (8 ounces) COOL WHIP® Whipped Topping, thawed
1 1/2 cups boiling water
1 package (8-serving size) or 2 packages (4-serving size each)
    JELL-O® Brand Gelatin, any flavor
1 can (15.25 ounces) pineapple cosmic fun shapes, drained,
    reserving juice
Ice cubes

SPOON about 1/3 cup of the whipped topping into each of 10 dessert dishes. Using back of spoon, spread whipped topping into bottom and up side of each dish. Refrigerate until ready to fill.

STIR boiling water into gelatin in large bowl at least 2 minutes until completely dissolved. Mix reserved juice and enough ice cubes to make 2 cups. Add to gelatin, stirring until slightly thickened (consistency of unbeaten egg whites). If necessary, refrigerate to thicken gelatin. Stir in pineapple fun shapes. Fill center of whipped topping with gelatin mixture.

REFRIGERATE 3 hours or until firm.          *Makes 10 servings*

**Preparation Time:** 15 minutes
**Refrigerating Time:** 3 hours

# Chocolate Passion Layered Dessert

4 cups cold milk

2 packages (4-serving size each) JELL-O® Chocolate Flavor
  Instant Pudding & Pie Filling

1 package (12 ounces) pound cake, cut into cubes

¼ cup chocolate syrup or coffee liqueur, divided

1 package (12 ounces) BAKER'S® Semi-Sweet Chocolate Chunks

1 tub (8 ounces) COOL WHIP® Extra Creamy Whipped
  Topping, thawed

POUR milk into large bowl. Add pudding mixes. Beat with wire whisk
1 minute or until well blended.

PLACE ½ of the cake cubes in large glass serving bowl. Drizzle with
½ of the chocolate syrup. Spread ½ of the pudding over cake in bowl.
Sprinkle ½ of the chunks over pudding. Spread with ½ of the whipped
topping. Repeat layers. Refrigerate until ready to serve.

*Makes 12 servings*

**Preparation Time:** 15 minutes

*Chocolate Passion Layered Dessert*

# JELL-O® Glazed Popcorn

    8 cups popped popcorn
    1 cup salted peanuts or cashews
 1/4 cup butter or margarine
    3 tablespoons light corn syrup
 1/2 cup packed light brown sugar or granulated sugar
    1 package (4-serving size) JELL-O® Brand Gelatin, any flavor

HEAT oven to 300°F. Line a 15×10×1-inch pan with foil or wax paper. Place popcorn and nuts in large bowl.

HEAT butter and syrup in small saucepan over low heat. Stir in sugar and gelatin; bring to a boil on medium heat. Reduce heat to low and gently simmer for 5 minutes. Immediately pour syrup over popcorn, tossing to coat well.

SPREAD popcorn in prepared pan, using two forks to spread evenly. Bake 10 minutes. Cool. Remove from pan and break into small pieces.

*Makes about 9 cups*

**Preparation Time:** 10 minutes
**Cooking Time:** 15 minutes

*JELL-O® Glazed Popcorn*

# Chocolate Candy Bar Dessert

 2 cups chocolate wafer cookie crumbs
$^1/_2$ cup sugar, divided
$^1/_2$ cup (1 stick) butter or margarine, melted
 1 package (8 ounces) PHILADELPHIA® Cream Cheese, softened
 1 tub (12 ounces) COOL WHIP® Whipped Topping, thawed
 1 cup chopped chocolate-covered candy bars
 3 cups cold milk
 2 packages (4-serving size) JELL-O® Chocolate Flavor Instant
 Pudding & Pie Filling

MIX cookie crumbs, $^1/_4$ cup of the sugar and butter in 13×9-inch pan. Press firmly onto bottom of pan. Refrigerate until ready to fill.

BEAT cream cheese and remaining $^1/_4$ cup sugar in medium bowl with wire whisk until smooth. Gently stir in $^1/_2$ of the whipped topping. Spread evenly over crust. Sprinkle chopped candy bars over cream cheese layer.

POUR milk into large bowl. Add pudding mixes. Beat with wire whisk 1 minute. Pour over chopped candy bar layer. Let stand 5 minutes or until thickened. Spread remaining whipped topping over pudding layer.

REFRIGERATE 2 hours or until set.          *Makes 15 servings*

**Preparation Time:** 25 minutes
**Refrigerating Time:** 2 hours

# Easy Pudding Milk Shake

>     3 cups cold milk
>     1 package (4-serving size) JELL-O® Instant Pudding & Pie
>         Filling, any flavor
>  1 1/2 cups ice cream, any flavor

POUR milk into blender container. Add pudding mix and ice cream; cover. Blend on high speed 30 seconds or until smooth. Pour into glasses and garnish as desired. Serve immediately. *Makes 5 servings*

**Preparation Time:** 5 minutes

*Easy Pudding Milk Shakes*

# Fruit 'n' Juice Squares

1 $1/2$ cups boiling water
1 package (8-serving size) or 2 packages (4-serving size each)
    JELL-O® Brand Strawberry or Cranberry Flavor Gelatin
1 cup cold orange juice
  Ice cubes
1 tub (8 ounces) COOL WHIP® Whipped Topping, thawed,
  divided
1 can (8$3/4$ ounces) fruit cocktail, drained

STIR boiling water into gelatin in large bowl at least 2 minutes until completely dissolved. Mix cold juice and ice cubes to make 1$1/4$ cups. Add to gelatin, stirring until slightly thickened (consistency of unbeaten egg whites). Remove any remaining ice. Refrigerate 45 minutes.

RESERVE 1 cup gelatin; set aside. Stir $1/2$ of the whipped topping into remaining gelatin until smooth. Pour mixture into 8-inch square pan. Refrigerate about 5 minutes until set but not firm (should stick to finger when touched and should mound). Stir fruit into reserved gelatin and carefully spoon over creamy layer in pan.

REFRIGERATE 3 hours or until firm. Cut into squares and garnish with remaining whipped topping. *Makes 9 servings*

**Storage Know How:** Keep gelatin refrigerated until ready to serve.

**Great Substitutes:** 1 cup seasonal fresh berries may be substituted for canned fruit.

**Preparation Time:** 15 minutes
**Refrigerating Time:** 3$3/4$ hours

*Fruit 'n' Juice Square*

# Peanut Butter-Banana Pops

1 package (16.1 ounces) JELL-O® No Bake Peanut Butter Cup
   Dessert
1 ⅓ cups cold milk
1 medium banana, chopped

PLACE Topping Pouch in large bowl of boiling water; set aside.

POUR milk into deep, medium bowl. Add Filling Mix and Peanut Butter Packet. Beat with electric mixer on lowest speed 30 seconds. Beat on highest speed 3 minutes. (Do not underbeat.) Gently stir in Crust Mix and banana. Spoon into 12 paper-lined muffin cups.

REMOVE pouch from water. Knead pouch 60 seconds until fluid and no longer lumpy. Squeeze topping equally over mixture in cups, tilting pan slightly to coat tops. Insert pop sticks into cups.

FREEZE 2 hours or overnight until firm. Remove paper liners.

*Makes 12 pops*

Note: Wooden pop sticks are sold at craft and hobby stores.

Preparation Time: 15 minutes
Freezing Time: 2 hours

*Peanut Butter-Banana Pops*

# Jell-O® Jigglers®

2½ cups boiling water or boiling apple juice (Do not add cold water or cold juice.)

2 packages (8-serving size) or 4 packages (4-serving size) JELL-O® Brand Gelatin Dessert, any flavor

STIR boiling water or boiling juice into gelatin in large bowl at least 3 minutes until completely dissolved. Pour into 13×9-inch pan.

REFRIGERATE 3 hours or until firm. Dip bottom of pan in warm water about 15 seconds. Cut into decorative shapes with cookie cutters all the way through gelatin or cut into 1-inch squares. Lift from pan.

*Makes about 24 pieces*

**Preparation Time:** 10 minutes
**Refrigerating Time:** 3 hours

# Ice Cream Pudding Pie

1 cup cold milk
1 cup ice cream (any flavor), softened
1 package (4-serving size) JELL-O® Instant Pudding & Pie Filling, any flavor
1 prepared graham cracker crumb crust (6 ounces)

MIX milk and ice cream in large bowl. Add pudding mix. Beat with electric mixer on lowest speed 1 minute. Pour immediately into crust.

REFRIGERATE 2 hours or until set.

*Makes 8 servings*

**Preparation Time:** 10 minutes
**Refrigerating Time:** 2 hours

# Yogurt Fluff

$^3/_4$ cup boiling water

1 package (4-serving size) JELL-O® Brand Sugar Free Low
Calorie Gelatin Dessert or JELL-O® Brand Gelatin Dessert,
any flavor

$^1/_2$ cup cold water or fruit juice

Ice cubes

1 container (8 ounces) BREYERS® Vanilla Lowfat Yogurt

$^1/_2$ teaspoon vanilla (optional)

5 tablespoons thawed COOL WHIP FREE® or COOL WHIP
LITE® Whipped Topping

STIR boiling water into gelatin in large bowl at least 2 minutes until
completely dissolved.

MIX cold water and ice cubes to make 1 cup. Add to gelatin, stirring until
slightly thickened. Remove any remaining ice. Stir in yogurt and vanilla.
Pour into dessert dishes.

REFRIGERATE 1$^1/_2$ hours or until firm. Top with whipped topping.

*Makes 5 servings*

**Preparation Time:** 10 minutes
**Refrigerating Time:** 1$^1/_2$ hours

# Family Favorites

Family meals are sure to be irresistible
when complemented with a sweet treat
from this collection. Most can be
whipped up in no time at all.

# Quick-and-Easy Holiday Trifle

    3 cups cold milk
    2 packages (4-serving size) JELL-O® Vanilla Flavor Instant
        Pudding & Pie Filling
    1 tub (8 ounces) COOL WHIP® Whipped Topping, thawed
    1 package (12 ounces) pound cake, cut into 1/2-inch cubes
 1/4 cup orange juice
    2 cups sliced strawberries

POUR milk into large bowl. Add pudding mixes. Beat with wire whisk
1 minute. Gently stir in 2 cups of the whipped topping.

ARRANGE 1/2 of the cake cubes in 31/2-quart serving bowl. Drizzle with
1/2 of the orange juice. Spoon 1/2 of the pudding mixture over cake cubes.
Top with strawberries. Layer with remaining cake cubes, orange juice and
pudding mixture.

REFRIGERATE until ready to serve. Top with remaining whipped
topping and garnish as desired.                    *Makes 12 servings*

**Preparation Time:** 20 minutes
**Refrigerating Time:** 1 hour

# Mocha Pudding Parfaits

1 1/2 cups cold fat-free milk

  1 tablespoon MAXWELL HOUSE® Instant Coffee

  1 package (4-serving size) JELL-O® Chocolate Flavor Fat Free
     Sugar Free Instant Reduced Calorie Pudding & Pie Filling

  1 tub (8 ounces) COOL WHIP FREE® Whipped Topping,
    thawed, divided

  6 reduced-fat chocolate wafer cookies, chopped

POUR milk and instant coffee into medium bowl. Add pudding mix. Beat with wire whisk 1 minute. Gently stir in 1/2 of the whipped topping.

SPOON 1/2 of the pudding mixture evenly into 6 dessert dishes. Sprinkle with chopped cookies.

COVER with 1/2 of the remaining whipped topping. Top with remaining pudding mixture. Garnish each serving with a spoonful of remaining whipped topping.

REFRIGERATE until ready to serve. *Makes 6 servings*

**Preparation Time:** 10 minutes

*Mocha Pudding Parfaits*

# Gelatin Pinwheels

**1 package (4-serving size) JELL-O® Brand Gelatin Dessert, any flavor**

**$^1/_2$ cup warm water**

**$1^1/_2$ cups miniature marshmallows or 12 large marshmallows**

SPRAY bottom and sides of 8- or 9-inch square pan lightly with no stick cooking spray.

MIX gelatin and water in $1^1/_2$- to 2-quart microwavable bowl. Microwave on HIGH $1^1/_2$ minutes; stir until completely dissolved. Add marshmallows. Microwave 1 minute or until marshmallows are puffed and almost melted. Remove from oven. Stir mixture slowly and gently until marshmallows are completely melted and mixture is smooth. (Creamy layer will float to top.) Pour into prepared pan.

REFRIGERATE 45 minutes or until set. Loosen edges with knife. Starting at 1 edge, roll up tightly. With seam-side down, cut into $^1/_2$-inch slices.

SERVE immediately or refrigerate until ready to serve.

*Makes 10 to 12 pieces*

**Preparation Time:** 10 minutes
**Refrigerating Time:** 45 minutes

# Pudding in a Cloud

    2 cups COOL WHIP® Whipped Topping, thawed
    2 cups cold milk
    1 package (4-serving size) JELL-O® Instant Pudding & Pie
        Filling, any flavor

SPOON whipped topping evenly into 6 dessert dishes. Using back of
spoon, make depression in center; spread whipped topping up side of each
dish.

POUR milk into medium bowl. Add pudding mix. Beat with wire whisk
2 minutes. Let stand 5 minutes. Spoon pudding into center of whipped
topping.

REFRIGERATE until ready to serve.                    *Makes 6 servings*

**Preparation Time:** 15 minutes
**Refrigerating Time:** 2 hours

# Berry Squares

 1 package (12 ounces) pound cake, cut into 10 slices
 3 tablespoons orange juice
 2 pints fresh seasonal berries (strawberries, raspberries or
     blueberries)
 2 tablespoons sugar
 2½ cups cold milk
 2 packages (4-serving size each) JELL-O® Vanilla or Lemon
     Flavor Instant Pudding & Pie Filling
 1 tub (8 ounces) COOL WHIP® Whipped Topping, thawed,
     divided

ARRANGE cake slices in bottom of 13×9-inch pan. Drizzle cake with juice. Top with berries; sprinkle with sugar.

POUR milk into large bowl. Add pudding mixes. Beat with wire whisk 1 minute or until well blended. Gently stir in 1 cup of the whipped topping. Spoon mixture over berries in pan. Top with remaining whipped topping.

REFRIGERATE until ready to serve or overnight. Garnish as desired.

*Makes 15 servings*

**Preparation Time:** 10 minutes

*Berry Square*

# Fudge Bottom Cheesecake

1 package (11.1 ounces) JELL-O® No Bake Real Cheesecake

2 tablespoons sugar

6 tablespoons butter or margarine, melted

1 tablespoon water

3 squares BAKER'S® Semi-Sweet Baking Chocolate

1 tablespoon butter or margarine

1 1/2 cups cold milk

STIR Crust Mix, sugar, melted butter and water thoroughly with fork in 9-inch pie plate until crumbs are well moistened. First press firmly against side of pie plate, using finger or measuring cup to shape edge. Press remaining crumbs firmly onto bottom, using measuring cup.

MICROWAVE chocolate and 1 tablespoon butter in small microwavable bowl on HIGH 1 1/2 minutes or until chocolate is almost melted. Stir until completely melted; cool slightly.

BEAT milk and Filling Mix with electric mixer on lowest speed until blended. Beat on medium speed 3 minutes. (Filling will be thick.) Stir 3 tablespoons of the filling into melted chocolate until well blended. Spread evenly into crust. Top with remaining filling.

REFRIGERATE at least 1 hour. Garnish as desired.

*Makes 8 servings*

**Fudge Bottom Cheesecake Tarts:** Using a spoon or bottom of glass, press prepared crust mixture firmly onto bottom of 12 paper-lined muffin cups. Prepare filling mixtures as directed above. Spread 1 heaping teaspoon of the chocolate mixture into each crust. Top with remaining filling. Refrigerate as directed.

**Tip:** For ease in serving, dip bottom of pie plate in hot water for 10 to 15 seconds prior to slicing.

**Preparation Time:** 15 minutes
**Refrigerating Time:** 1 hour

# Cranberry-Orange Cooler

   1 cup boiling water
   1 package (4-serving size) JELL-O® Brand Orange Flavor Gelatin
2$^1/_2$ cups cranberry juice, chilled
    Ice cubes (optional)
    Orange slices (optional)

**STIR** boiling water into gelatin in large bowl at least 2 minutes until completely dissolved. Add cranberry juice. Pour over ice cubes in tall glasses and garnish with orange slices, if desired.

*Makes about 3$^1/_2$ cups*

**Preparation Time:** 5 minutes

# 5 Minute Mousse

1½ cups cold milk

1 package (4-serving size) JELL-O® Instant Pudding & Pie
    Filling, any flavor

1½ cups thawed COOL WHIP® Whipped Topping

POUR milk into large bowl. Add pudding mix. Beat with wire whisk
2 minutes.

STIR in 1 cup of the whipped topping. Spoon into individual dessert
dishes or serving bowl.

REFRIGERATE until ready to serve. Top with remaining whipped
topping and garnish as desired. *Makes 5 servings*

**Low Fat Pudding Mousse:** Prepare recipe as directed above using skim
milk, any flavor JELL-O® Fat Free Sugar Free Instant Reduced Calorie
Pudding & Pie Filling and COOL WHIP FREE® or COOL WHIP
LITE® Whipped Topping.

**Preparation Time:** 5 minutes
**Refrigerating Time:** 2 hours

*5 Minute Mousse*

# Tropical Terrine

    1 package (3 ounces) ladyfingers, split, divided
1 1/2 cups boiling water
    1 package (8-serving size) or 2 packages (4-serving size) JELL-O®
        Brand Orange Flavor Sugar Free Low Calorie Gelatin
        Dessert
    1 can (8 ounces) crushed pineapple in juice, undrained
    1 cup cold water
    2 cups thawed COOL WHIP LITE® Whipped Topping
    1 can (11 ounces) mandarin orange segments, drained
      Additional thawed COOL WHIP LITE® Whipped Topping
      Kiwi slices
      Star fruit slices
      Pineapple leaves

LINE bottom and sides of 9×5-inch loaf pan with plastic wrap. Add enough ladyfingers, cut sides in, to fit evenly along all sides of pan.

STIR boiling water into gelatin in large bowl 2 minutes or until completely dissolved. Stir in pineapple with juice and cold water. Refrigerate 1 1/4 hours or until slightly thickened (consistency of unbeaten egg whites). Gently stir in 2 cups whipped topping and oranges. Spoon into prepared pan. Arrange remaining ladyfingers, cut sides down, evenly on top of gelatin mixture.

REFRIGERATE 3 hours or until firm. Place serving plate on top of pan. Invert, holding pan and plate together; shake gently to loosen. Carefully remove pan and plastic wrap. Garnish with additional whipped topping, fruit and pineapple leaves. *Makes 12 servings*

*Tropical Terrine*

# Berried Delight

1$\frac{1}{2}$ cups graham cracker crumbs

$\frac{1}{2}$ cup sugar, divided

$\frac{1}{2}$ cup (1 stick) butter or margarine, melted

1 package (8 ounces) PHILADELPHIA® Cream Cheese, softened

2 tablespoons milk

1 tub (8 ounces) COOL WHIP® Whipped Topping, thawed

2 pints strawberries, hulled, halved

3$\frac{1}{2}$ cups cold milk

2 packages (4-serving size) JELL-O® Vanilla Flavor Instant
    Pudding & Pie Filling

MIX crumbs, $\frac{1}{4}$ cup of the sugar and butter in 13×9-inch pan. Press firmly onto bottom of pan. Refrigerate until ready to fill.

*Berried Delight*

BEAT cream cheese, remaining $1/4$ cup sugar and 2 tablespoons milk until smooth. Gently stir in $1/2$ of the whipped topping. Spread over crust. Top with strawberry halves.

POUR $3^1/2$ cups milk into large bowl. Add pudding mixes. Beat with wire whisk 2 minutes. Pour over cream cheese layer.

REFRIGERATE 4 hours or until set. Just before serving, spread remaining whipped topping over pudding.           *Makes 15 servings*

**Preparation Time:** 30 minutes
**Refrigerating Time:** 4 hours

# Strawberry Banana Salad

   $1^1/2$ **cups boiling water**
   **1 package (8-serving size) or 2 packages (4-serving size each)**
       **JELL-O® Brand Strawberry or Strawberry Banana Flavor**
       **Sugar Free Low Calorie Gelatin**
   **2 cups cold water**
   **1 cup chopped strawberries**
   **1 banana, sliced**

STIR boiling water into gelatin in large bowl at least 2 minutes until completely dissolved. Stir in cold water. Refrigerate about $1^1/2$ hours or until thickened (spoon drawn through leaves definite impression).

STIR in strawberries and banana. Pour into 5-cup mold that has been sprayed with no stick cooking spray. Refrigerate 4 hours or until firm. Unmold. Store leftover gelatin mold in refrigerator.

           *Makes 10 ($1/2$-cup) servings*

**Preparation Time:** 15 minutes
**Refrigerating Time:** $5^1/2$ hours

# Chocolate Peanut Butter Parfaits

3 tablespoons milk

3 tablespoons peanut butter

1 cup thawed COOL WHIP® Whipped Topping

2 cups cold milk

1 package (4-serving size) JELL-O® Chocolate Flavor Instant
Pudding & Pie Filling

$1/4$ cup chopped peanuts

STIR 3 tablespoons milk into peanut butter in medium bowl until smooth. Gently stir in whipped topping.

POUR 2 cups milk into medium bowl. Add pudding mix. Beat with wire whisk 2 minutes. Alternately spoon whipped topping mixture and pudding into 6 parfait glasses.

REFRIGERATE until ready to serve. Sprinkle with peanuts.

*Makes 6 servings*

**Preparation Time:** 5 minutes

90

*Chocolate Peanut Butter Parfaits*

# Fruity JELL-O® Cake

2 cups chopped strawberries

1 can (20 ounces) crushed pineapple, drained

1 package (8-serving size) or 2 packages (4-serving size each)
   JELL-O® Brand Strawberry Flavor Gelatin

3 cups miniature marshmallows

1 package (2-layer size) white cake mix

2 eggs

HEAT oven to 350°F.

ARRANGE fruit on bottom of 13×9-inch pan. Sprinkle with gelatin.
Cover with marshmallows.

PREPARE cake mix as directed on package, omitting oil and using
2 eggs and water as specified. Spread batter over mixture in pan.

BAKE 50 to 55 minutes. Remove to rack; cool 15 minutes. Serve warm
with thawed COOL WHIP Whipped Topping, if desired.

*Makes 24 servings*

**Preparation Time:** 15 minutes

**Baking Time:** 55 minutes

*Fruity JELL-O® Cake*

# Dynamic Desserts

*You don't have to wait for a birthday or holiday to make one of these exciting desserts. Any meal becomes a celebration with these delicious treats.*

# Merry Cherry Holiday Dessert

1 1/2 cups boiling water

1 package (8-serving size) or 2 packages (4-serving size) JELL-O® Brand Cherry Flavor Gelatin Dessert, or any red flavor

1 1/2 cups cold water

1 can (21 ounces) cherry pie filling

4 cups angel food cake cubes

3 cups cold milk

2 packages (4-serving size) JELL-O® Vanilla Flavor Instant Pudding & Pie Filling

1 tub (8 ounces) COOL WHIP® Whipped Topping, thawed

STIR boiling water into gelatin in large bowl at least 2 minutes until completely dissolved. Stir in cold water and cherry pie filling. Refrigerate about 1 hour or until slightly thickened (consistency of unbeaten egg whites). Place cake cubes in 3-quart serving bowl. Spoon gelatin mixture over cake. Refrigerate about 45 minutes or until set but not firm (gelatin should stick to finger when touched and should mound).

POUR milk into large bowl. Add pudding mixes. Beat with wire whisk 1 minute. Gently stir in 2 cups of the whipped topping. Spoon over gelatin mixture in bowl.

REFRIGERATE 2 hours or until set. Top with remaining whipped topping and garnish as desired. *Makes 16 servings*

**Preparation Time:** 20 minutes
**Refrigerating Time:** 3 3/4 hours

# Holiday Poke Cake

2 baked 8- or 9-inch round white cake layers, cooled completely

2 cups boiling water

1 package (4-serving size) JELL-O® Brand Gelatin Dessert, any red flavor

1 package (4-serving size) JELL-O® Brand Lime Flavor Gelatin Dessert

1 tub (8 or 12 ounces) COOL WHIP® Whipped Topping, thawed

PLACE cake layers, top sides up, in 2 clean 8- or 9-inch round cake pans. Pierce cake with large fork at ½-inch intervals.

STIR 1 cup of the boiling water into each flavor of gelatin in separate bowls at least 2 minutes until completely dissolved. Carefully pour red gelatin over 1 cake layer and lime gelatin over second cake layer. Refrigerate 3 hours.

DIP 1 cake pan in warm water 10 seconds; unmold onto serving plate. Spread with about 1 cup of the whipped topping. Unmold second cake layer; carefully place on first cake layer. Frost top and side of cake with remaining whipped topping.

REFRIGERATE at least 1 hour or until ready to serve. Decorate as desired.                                                                 *Makes 12 servings*

**Preparation Time:** 30 minutes
**Refrigerating Time:** 4 hours

# Lemon Bars

15 whole graham crackers

2 packages (8 ounces each) PHILADELPHIA® Cream Cheese, softened

3½ cups cold milk

3 packages (4-serving size each) JELL-O® Lemon Flavor Instant Pudding & Pie Filling

1 tub (8 ounces) COOL WHIP® Whipped Topping, thawed, divided

ARRANGE ½ of the crackers in bottom of 13×9-inch pan, cutting crackers to fit, if necessary.

BEAT cream cheese in large bowl with electric mixer on low speed until smooth. Gradually beat in 1 cup of the milk. Add remaining milk and pudding mixes. Beat 1 to 2 minutes. (Mixture will be thick.) Gently stir in 2 cups of the whipped topping.

SPREAD ½ of the pudding mixture over crackers in pan. Arrange remaining crackers over pudding in pan. Top with remaining pudding mixture. Cover with remaining whipped topping. Refrigerate 4 hours or freeze 3 hours. Cut into bars.                    *Makes 18 servings*

**Preparation Time:** 10 minutes
**Refrigerating Time:** 4 hours
**Freezing Time:** 3 hours

# Florida Sunshine Cups

 $^3/_4$ cup boiling water

 1 package (4-serving size) JELL-O® Brand Orange or Lemon
    Flavor Sugar Free Low Calorie Gelatin

 1 cup cold orange juice

 $^1/_2$ cup fresh raspberries

 1 can (11 ounces) mandarin orange segments, drained

STIR boiling water into gelatin in large bowl at least 2 minutes until completely dissolved. Stir in cold juice. Refrigerate $1^1/_2$ hours or until thickened (spoon drawn through leaves definite impression).

MEASURE $^3/_4$ cup thickened gelatin into medium bowl; set aside. Stir fruit into remaining gelatin. Pour into serving bowl or 6 dessert dishes.

BEAT reserved gelatin with electric mixer on high speed until fluffy and about doubled in volume. Spoon over gelatin in bowl or dishes.

REFRIGERATE 3 hours or until firm.                    *Makes 6 servings*

**Preparation Time:**  20 minutes
**Refrigerating Time:** $4^1/_2$ hours

*Florida Sunshine Cups*

# Orange Pineapple Layered Dessert

1 1/2 cups boiling water

1 package (8-serving size) or 2 packages (4-serving size) JELL-O®
   Brand Orange Flavor Gelatin Dessert

1 cup cold water

1 can (20 ounces) crushed pineapple in juice, undrained

1 can (11 ounces) mandarin orange segments, drained

1 1/2 cups graham cracker crumbs

1/2 cup sugar, divided

1/2 cup (1 stick) butter or margarine, melted

1 package (8 ounces) PHILADELPHIA® Cream Cheese, softened

2 tablespoons milk

1 tub (8 ounces) COOL WHIP® Whipped Topping, thawed

STIR boiling water into gelatin in large bowl at least 2 minutes until completely dissolved. Stir in cold water, pineapple with juice and oranges. Refrigerate about 1 1/4 hours or until slightly thickened (consistency of unbeaten egg whites).

MIX crumbs, 1/4 cup of the sugar and butter in 13×9-inch pan. Press firmly onto bottom of pan. Refrigerate until ready to fill.

BEAT cream cheese, remaining 1/4 cup sugar and milk in large bowl until smooth. Gently stir in 2 cups of the whipped topping. Spread evenly over crust. Spoon gelatin over cream cheese layer.

REFRIGERATE 3 hours or until firm. Garnish with remaining whipped topping.  *Makes 15 servings*

**Preparation Time:** 30 minutes
**Refrigerating Time:** 4 1/4 hours

# 15 Minute Vanilla Rice Pudding

    3 cups milk, divided
    1 cup MINUTE® White Rice, uncooked
    1/3 cup raisins (optional)
    1 package (4-serving size) JELL-O® Vanilla Flavor Instant
        Pudding & Pie Filling

BOIL 1 cup milk in medium saucepan. Stir in rice and raisins; cover.
Remove from heat. Let stand 5 minutes.

MEANWHILE, prepare pudding as directed on package with remaining
2 cups milk.

ADD rice mixture to prepared pudding; stir. Cover surface of pudding
with plastic wrap; cool 5 minutes. Stir. Serve warm or chilled. Sprinkle
with cinnamon, if desired.                              *Makes 6 servings*

**Tip:** To add a springtime touch, omit cinnamon.  Sprinkle with tinted
BAKER'S® ANGEL FLAKE® Coconut  and pastel miniature jelly beans.
To tint coconut, dilute a few drops of green food coloring with 1/2 teaspoon
water. Add to 1 cup coconut in small zipper-style plastic bag. Shake until
coconut is evenly tinted.

**Variation:** Substitute skim milk for 2% milk.

# Easy Eclair Dessert

27 whole graham crackers, halved
3 cups cold milk
2 packages (4-serving size) JELL-O® Vanilla Flavor Instant
    Pudding & Pie Filling
1 tub (12 ounces) COOL WHIP® Whipped Topping, thawed
1 container (16 ounces) ready-to-spread chocolate fudge frosting
Strawberries

ARRANGE ⅓ of the crackers on bottom of 13×9-inch baking pan, breaking crackers to fit, if necessary.

POUR milk into large bowl. Add pudding mixes. Beat with wire whisk 2 minutes. Gently stir in whipped topping. Spread ½ of the pudding mixture over crackers. Place ½ of the remaining crackers over pudding; top with remaining pudding mixture and crackers.

*Easy Eclair Dessert*

REMOVE top and foil from frosting container. Microwave frosting in container on HIGH 1 minute or until pourable. Spread evenly over crackers.

REFRIGERATE 4 hours or overnight. Cut into squares to serve. Garnish with strawberries. *Makes 18 servings*

**Tip:** You could make pistachio, banana-flavored or even double chocolate eclairs by simply changing the pudding flavors.

**Preparation Time:** 20 minutes
**Refrigerating Time:** 4 hours

# Black Forest Parfaits

2 cups cold skim milk
4 ounces PHILADELPHIA® Neufchâtel Cheese
1 package (4-serving size) JELL-O® Chocolate Flavor Fat Free
    Sugar Free Instant Reduced Calorie Pudding & Pie Filling
1 can (20 ounces) reduced calorie cherry pie filling
3 cups fat free chocolate pound cake cubes (½ loaf)
1 square BAKER'S® Semi-Sweet Chocolate, grated

Pour ½ cup of the cold milk into blender container. Add cheese; cover. Blend on medium speed until smooth. Add remaining cold milk and pudding mix; cover. Blend until smooth.

Divide cake cubes evenly among 8 dessert dishes. Spoon pudding mixture then cherries over cake cubes, reserving a few cherries for garnish. Top with pudding mixture. Refrigerate until ready to serve. Garnish with reserved cherries and chocolate. *Makes 8 servings*

# Fresh Fruit Parfaits

1 cup fresh fruit

¾ cup boiling water

1 package (4-serving size) JELL-O® Brand Sugar Free
    Low Calorie Gelatin Dessert or JELL-O® Brand Gelatin
    Dessert, any flavor

½ cup cold water
    Ice cubes

¾ cup thawed COOL WHIP FREE® or COOL WHIP LITE®
    Whipped Topping

DIVIDE fruit among 6 parfait glasses.

STIR boiling water into gelatin in medium bowl at least 2 minutes until completely dissolved. Mix cold water and ice cubes to make 1¼ cups. Add to gelatin, stirring until slightly thickened. Remove any remaining ice. Measure ¾ cup of the gelatin; pour into parfait glasses. Refrigerate 1 hour or until set but not firm (gelatin should stick to finger when touched and should mound).

STIR whipped topping into remaining gelatin with wire whisk until smooth. Spoon over gelatin in glasses.

REFRIGERATE 1 hour or until firm. Garnish as desired.

*Makes 6 servings*

**Preparation Time:** 20 minutes
**Refrigerating Time:** 2 hours

*Fresh Fruit Parfaits*

# Café Ladyfinger Dessert

2 packages (3 ounces each) ladyfingers, split
1 cup freshly brewed strong MAXWELL HOUSE® or YUBAN®
    Coffee, any variety, at room temperature, divided
1 package (8 ounces) PHILADELPHIA FREE® Fat Free
    Cream Cheese
2 cups cold fat free milk
2 packages (4-serving size each) JELL-O® Vanilla Flavor Fat Free
    Sugar Free Instant Reduced Calorie Pudding & Pie Filling
1 tub (8 ounces) COOL WHIP FREE® Whipped Topping,
    thawed, divided

BRUSH cut side of ladyfingers with about ¼ cup of the coffee. Place ladyfingers on bottom and up side of 2-quart serving bowl.

BEAT cream cheese and remaining ¾ cup coffee in large bowl with wire whisk until smooth. Gradually beat in milk until smooth. Add pudding mixes. Beat with wire whisk 1 minute or until well blended. Gently stir in ½ of the whipped topping. Spoon into prepared bowl; cover.

REFRIGERATE 1 hour or until ready to serve. Top with remaining whipped topping. *Makes 12 servings*

**Special Extra:** Garnish with 3 tablespoons shaved or chopped chocolate.

**Preparation Time:** 20 minutes
**Refrigerating Time:** 1 hour

*Café Ladyfinger Dessert*

# Pastel Swirl Dessert

1 package (3 ounces) ladyfingers, split
1⅓ cups boiling water
2 packages (4-serving size) JELL-O® Brand Gelatin Dessert, any
    2 different flavors
1 cup cold water
    Ice cubes
1 tub (12 ounces) COOL WHIP® Whipped Topping, thawed

TRIM about 1 inch off 1 end of each ladyfinger; reserve trimmed ends.
Place ladyfingers, cut ends down, around side of 9-inch springform pan.*
Place trimmed ends on bottom of pan.

STIR ⅔ cup of the boiling water into each package of gelatin in separate
medium bowls at least 2 minutes until completely dissolved. Mix cold
water and ice cubes to make 2½ cups. Stir ½ of the ice water into each
bowl until gelatin is slightly thickened. Remove any remaining ice.

GENTLY stir ½ of the whipped topping with wire whisk into each
gelatin mixture until smooth. Refrigerate 20 to 30 minutes or until
mixtures are very thick and will mound. Spoon mixtures alternately into
prepared pan. Swirl with knife to marbleize.

REFRIGERATE 4 hours or until firm. Remove side of pan.

*Makes 16 servings*

*To prepare in 13×9-inch pan, do not trim ladyfingers. Line bottom of pan with ladyfingers.
Continue as directed.*

**Preparation Time:** 30 minutes
**Refrigerating Time:** 4½ hours

*Pastel Swirl Dessert*

# Double Chocolate Bread Pudding

5 cups milk

2 packages (4-serving size) JELL-O® Chocolate Fudge Flavor
Cook & Serve Pudding & Pie Filling *(not Instant)*

5 cups cubed French bread

1 cup BAKER'S® Semi-Sweet Real Chocolate Chips

HEAT oven to 350°F.

POUR milk into large bowl. Add pudding mixes. Beat with wire whisk
1 minute. Stir in bread. Pour pudding mixture into 13×9-inch baking
dish. Sprinkle evenly with chocolate chips.

BAKE 45 minutes or until mixture comes to boil. Remove from oven.
Let stand 10 minutes. Serve warm. *Makes 15 servings*

**Preparation Time:** 15 minutes
**Baking Time:** 45 minutes

# Creamy Lemon Bars

1 1/2 cups graham cracker crumbs

1/2 cup sugar, divided

1/2 cup (1 stick) butter or margarine, melted

1 package (8 ounces) PHILADELPHIA® Cream Cheese, softened

2 tablespoons milk

1 tub (8 ounces) COOL WHIP® Whipped Topping, thawed

1 package (4.3 ounces) JELL-O® Lemon Flavor Cook & Serve
    Pudding & Pie Filling *(not Instant)*

3/4 cup sugar

3 cups water, divided

3 egg yolks

MIX crumbs, 1/4 cup of the sugar and butter in 13×9-inch pan. Press
firmly onto bottom of pan. Refrigerate until ready to fill.

BEAT cream cheese, remaining 1/4 cup sugar and milk until smooth.
Gently stir in 1/2 of the whipped topping. Spread evenly over crust.

STIR pudding mix, 3/4 cup sugar, 1/2 cup of the water and egg yolks in
medium saucepan. Stir in remaining 2 1/2 cups water. Stirring constantly,
cook on medium heat until mixture comes to full boil. Cool 5 minutes,
stirring twice. Pour over cream cheese layer.

REFRIGERATE 4 hours or until set. Just before serving, spread
remaining whipped topping over pudding.           *Makes 15 servings*

**Preparation Time:** 25 minutes
**Refrigerating Time:** 4 hours

# Chocolate Toffee Bar Dessert

1 cup flour

$^1/_2$ cup pecans, toasted and finely chopped

$^1/_4$ cup sugar

$^1/_2$ cup (1 stick) butter or margarine, melted

1 cup toffee bits, divided

2 cups cold milk

2 packages (4-serving size each) JELL-O® Chocolate Flavor Instant Pudding & Pie Filling

1 tub (8 ounces) COOL WHIP® Whipped Topping, thawed, divided

HEAT oven to 400°F.

MIX flour, pecans, sugar, butter and $^1/_2$ cup of the toffee bits in large bowl until well mixed. Press firmly onto bottom of 13×9-inch pan. Bake 10 minutes or until lightly browned. Cool.

POUR milk into large bowl. Add pudding mixes. Beat with wire whisk 1 minute or until well blended. Spread $1^1/_2$ cups pudding on bottom of crust.

GENTLY stir $^1/_2$ of the whipped topping into remaining pudding. Spread over pudding in pan. Top with remaining whipped topping. Sprinkle with remaining toffee bits.

REFRIGERATE 3 hours or overnight.                    *Makes 15 servings*

**Preparation Time:** 20 minutes
**Baking Time:** 10 minutes
**Refrigerating Time:** 3 hours

*Chocolate Toffee Bar Dessert*

# Creamy Vanilla Sauce

3½ cups cold milk, light cream or half-and-half
1 package (4-serving size) JELL-O® Vanilla or French Vanilla
Flavor Instant Pudding & Pie Filling

POUR milk into bowl. Add pudding mix. Beat with wire whisk 2 minutes.
Cover.

REFRIGERATE until ready to serve. Serve over your favorite fruits or
cake. Garnish as desired. *Makes 3½ cups*

**Creamy Citrus Sauce:** Add 2 teaspoons grated orange peel with pudding
mix.

**Preparation Time:** 5 minutes

*Creamy Vanilla Sauce*

# Apple Walnut Bread Pudding

    4 cups cubed French bread
    3 medium apples, chopped
    1 cup chopped walnuts
    4 cups milk
    2 packages (4-serving size) JELL-O® Vanilla Flavor Cook & Serve
        Pudding & Pie Filling *(not Instant)*
    2 teaspoons ground cinnamon, divided

HEAT oven to 350°F.

PLACE bread cubes in lightly greased 13×9-inch baking dish. Add apples and walnuts; toss to mix well.

POUR milk into large bowl. Add pudding mixes and 1 teaspoon of the cinnamon. Beat with wire whisk 1 minute. Pour over bread mixture; sprinkle top with remaining cinnamon.

BAKE 50 to 60 minutes or until mixture comes to boil. Remove from oven. Let stand 10 minutes before serving. Serve warm.

*Makes 15 servings*

**Preparation Time:** 20 minutes
**Baking Time:** 1 hour

# Tiramisu

    1 package (3 ounces) ladyfingers, split
1 1/2 cups cold skim milk, divided
    1 container (8 ounces) PHILADELPHIA LIGHT® Soft Light
        Cream Cheese
    2 tablespoons MAXWELL HOUSE® Instant Coffee
    1 tablespoon hot water
    2 tablespoons brandy (optional)
    1 package (4-serving size) JELL-O® Brand Vanilla Flavor Fat Free
        Sugar Free Instant Reduced Calorie Pudding & Pie Filling
    2 cups thawed COOL WHIP LITE® Whipped Topping
    1 square (1 ounce) BAKER'S® Semi-Sweet Baking Chocolate,
        grated

CUT ladyfingers in half horizontally. Cover bottom of 8-inch springform pan with ladyfinger halves. Place remaining ladyfinger halves, cut ends down, around sides of pan.

PLACE 1/2 cup cold milk and cream cheese in blender container; cover. Blend on medium speed until smooth. Dissolve coffee in hot water. Place in blender container with brandy and remaining 1 cup cold milk. Add pudding mix; cover. Blend until smooth. Pour into large bowl.

STIR in whipped topping immediately. Spoon pudding mixture into pan.

REFRIGERATE 4 hours or until set. Remove sides of pan. Garnish with chocolate.                                                 *Makes 12 servings*

**Preparation Time:** 20 minutes
**Refrigerating Time** 4 hours

*Tiramisu*

# Striped Delight

35 chocolate sandwich cookies, finely crushed (3 cups)
6 tablespoons butter or margarine, melted
1 package (8 ounces) PHILADELPHIA® Cream cheese, softened
$^1/_4$ cup sugar
2 tablespoons cold milk
1 tub (12 ounces) COOL WHIP® Whipped Topping, thawed
3$^1/_4$ cups cold milk
2 packages (4-serving size) JELL-O® Chocolate Flavor Instant
     Pudding & Pie Filling

MIX crushed cookies and butter in medium bowl. Press firmly into bottom of foil-lined 13×9-inch pan. Refrigerate 15 minutes.

BEAT cream cheese, sugar and 2 tablespoons milk in medium bowl with wire whisk until smooth. Gently stir in 1$^1/_4$ cups of the whipped topping. Spread over crust.

POUR 3$^1/_4$ cups milk into large bowl. Add pudding mixes. Beat with wire whisk 1 to 2 minutes. Pour over cream cheese layer. Let stand 5 minutes or until thickened. Drop remaining whipped topping by spoonfuls over pudding. Spread to cover pudding.

REFRIGERATE 4 hours or overnight. Cut into squares.

*Makes 16 servings*

**Tip:** For easier cutting, place dessert in freezer 1 hour before serving.

**Preparation Time:** 20 minutes
**Refrigerating Time:** 4 hours 15 minutes

*Striped Delight*

# Fruity Gelatin Pops

> 1 cup boiling water
> 1 package (4-serving size) JELL-O® Brand Gelatin Dessert, any flavor
> $1/3$ cup sugar
> $1\,1/3$ cups cold juice, any flavor
> 6 (5-ounce) paper cups

STIR boiling water into gelatin and sugar in medium bowl at least 2 minutes until completely dissolved. Stir in cold juice. Pour into cups. Freeze about 2 hours or until almost firm. Insert wooden pop stick into each for handle.

FREEZE 5 hours or overnight until firm. To remove pop from cup, place bottom of cup under warm running water for 15 seconds. Press firmly on bottom of cup to release pop. (Do not twist or pull pop stick.) Store leftover pops in freezer up to 2 weeks. *Makes 6 pops*

**Outrageous Orange Pops:** Use 1 cup boiling water, JELL-O® Brand Orange Flavor Gelatin Dessert, $1/3$ cup sugar and $1\,1/3$ cups orange juice.

**Fruity Strawberry Pops:** Use 1 cup boiling water, JELL-O® Brand Strawberry Flavor Gelatin Dessert, $1/3$ cup sugar, $2/3$ cup cold water and $2/3$ cup puréed strawberries.

**Fizzy Grape Pops:** Use 1 cup boiling water, JELL-O® Brand Sparkling White Grape Flavor Gelatin Dessert, 2 tablespoons sugar and $1\,1/2$ cups carbonated grape beverage.

**Lemonade Pops:** Use 1 cup boiling water, JELL-O® Brand Lemon Flavor Gelatin Dessert, ¹/₃ cup sugar, 1 cup cold water and 2 tablespoons lemon juice.

**Iced Tea Pops:** Use 1 cup boiling water, JELL-O® Brand Lemon Flavor Gelatin Dessert, 2 tablespoons sugar and 1¹/₂ cups pre-sweetened iced tea.

**Preparation Time:** 10 minutes
**Freezing Time:** 7 hours

*Fruity Gelatin Pops*

# Chocolate Banana Parfaits

2 cups cold fat free milk

1 package (4-serving size) JELL-O® Chocolate Flavor Fat Free
    Sugar Free Instant Reduced Calorie Pudding & Pie Filling

2 medium bananas, sliced

1/2 cup thawed COOL WHIP LITE® Whipped Topping

1 tablespoon chopped walnuts

POUR milk into medium bowl. Add pudding mix. Beat with wire whisk
1 minute.

SPOON 1/2 of the pudding evenly into 4 dessert glasses. Layer with
banana slices, whipped topping and remaining pudding.

REFRIGERATE until ready to serve. Garnish each serving with
additional banana slices, whipped topping and walnuts, if desired.

*Makes 4 servings*

**Great Substitute:** For a really great twist, prepare as directed above,
substituting JELL-O® Vanilla Flavor Fat Free Sugar Free Instant
Reduced Calorie Pudding & Pie Filling for the Chocolate Flavor and
drizzle each serving with 1 teaspoon KRAFT® Caramel Topping.

**Preparation Time:** 5 minutes

# INDEX

# METRIC CONVERSION CHART

### VOLUME MEASUREMENTS (dry)

$1/8$ teaspoon = 0.5 mL
$1/4$ teaspoon = 1 mL
$1/2$ teaspoon = 2 mL
$3/4$ teaspoon = 4 mL
1 teaspoon = 5 mL
1 tablespoon = 15 mL
2 tablespoons = 30 mL
$1/4$ cup = 60 mL
$1/3$ cup = 75 mL
$1/2$ cup = 125 mL
$2/3$ cup = 150 mL
$3/4$ cup = 175 mL
1 cup = 250 mL
2 cups = 1 pint = 500 mL
3 cups = 750 mL
4 cups = 1 quart = 1 L

### VOLUME MEASUREMENTS (fluid)

1 fluid ounce (2 tablespoons) = 30 mL
4 fluid ounces ($1/2$ cup) = 125 mL
8 fluid ounces (1 cup) = 250 mL
12 fluid ounces ($1 1/2$ cups) = 375 mL
16 fluid ounces (2 cups) = 500 mL

### WEIGHTS (mass)

$1/2$ ounce = 15 g
1 ounce = 30 g
3 ounces = 90 g
4 ounces = 120 g
8 ounces = 225 g
10 ounces = 285 g
12 ounces = 360 g
16 ounces = 1 pound = 450 g

### DIMENSIONS

$1/16$ inch = 2 mm
$1/8$ inch = 3 mm
$1/4$ inch = 6 mm
$1/2$ inch = 1.5 cm
$3/4$ inch = 2 cm
1 inch = 2.5 cm

### OVEN TEMPERATURES

250°F = 120°C
275°F = 140°C
300°F = 150°C
325°F = 160°C
350°F = 180°C
375°F = 190°C
400°F = 200°C
425°F = 220°C
450°F = 230°C

### BAKING PAN SIZES

| Utensil | Size in Inches/Quarts | Metric Volume | Size in Centimeters |
|---|---|---|---|
| Baking or | $8 \times 8 \times 2$ | 2 L | $20 \times 20 \times 5$ |
| Cake Pan | $9 \times 9 \times 2$ | 2.5 L | $23 \times 23 \times 5$ |
| (square or | $12 \times 8 \times 2$ | 3 L | $30 \times 20 \times 5$ |
| rectangular) | $13 \times 9 \times 2$ | 3.5 L | $33 \times 23 \times 5$ |
| Loaf Pan | $8 \times 4 \times 3$ | 1.5 L | $20 \times 10 \times 7$ |
| | $9 \times 5 \times 3$ | 2 L | $23 \times 13 \times 7$ |
| Round Layer | $8 \times 1 1/2$ | 1.2 L | $20 \times 4$ |
| Cake Pan | $9 \times 1 1/2$ | 1.5 L | $23 \times 4$ |
| Pie Plate | $8 \times 1 1/4$ | 750 mL | $20 \times 3$ |
| | $9 \times 1 1/4$ | 1 L | $23 \times 3$ |
| Baking Dish | 1 quart | 1 L | — |
| or Casserole | $1 1/2$ quart | 1.5 L | — |
| | 2 quart | 2 L | — |